Writers' Secrets

NIKKI GAMBLE

WAYLAND

First published in 2008 by Wayland

Copyright © Wayland 2008

Wayland
338 Euston Road
London NW1 3BH

Wayland Australia
Hachette Children's Books
Level 17/207 Kent Street
Sydney, NSW 2000

Design: Rawshock Design
Managing Designer: Paul Cherrill
Picture Researcher: Shelley Noronha

British Library Cataloguing in Publication Data

Gamble, Nikki
    Writers' secrets
    1. Novelists, English - Interviews - Juvenile
    literature
    2. Fiction - Technique - Juvenile literature 3.
    Fiction - Authorship - Juvenile literature
    I. Title
    808.3

ISBN 9780750253703

Printed in China

Wayland is a division of Hachette Children's Books,
an Hachette Livre UK company.

www.hachettelivre.co.uk

The publisher would like to thank the following for permission to reproduce their pictures:
Cover of *Grk and the Hot Dog Trail* used by permission of Anderson Press Ltd 21; © 81A Productions/Corbis 14; © Richard Cummins/Corbis 13; © John Harper/Corbis 11; © Image Source/Corbis 22; © Serge Kozak/zefa/Corbis 24; © Anatoly Maltsev/epa/Corbis 12; © Andersen Ross/Blend Images/Corbis 5; © Sally Taylor by permission of Catnip Publishing Ltd 19; HarperCollins Publishers Ltd © 2006 Michael Carroll 8; Cover of *Thomas Trew and the Hidden People* used by permission of Hodder Children's Books, a division of Hodder and Stoughton Ltd 9; Cover of *Star Dancer* by Beth Webb courtesy of Macmillan Children's Books, London, UK 25; Cover of *Happy Ever After: Red Riding Hood Takes Charge* used by permission of Orchard Books, a division of Watts Publishing Group Ltd 16; Front cover from *Dictionary of English Surnames* by Reaney PH (1998) By permission of Oxford University Press 18; Penguin UK 23; © Ute Klaphake/Photofusion 17; Cover of *Rescuing Dad* used by permission of The Random House Group Ltd 21; Chad Ehlers /Stock Connection/Rex Features 7; Dezo Hoffmann/Rex Features 26; Geoffrey Swaine/Rex Features 27; Ray Tang / Rex Features cover, 4; The Travel Library/Rex Features 10; Geoff Wilkinson/Rex Features 6; John Kanellopoulos/Rex Features 15.
Extract from *Rescuing Dad* by Pete Johnson published by Corgi Yearling. Reprinted by permission of The Random House Group Ltd.
Extract from *Grk and the Hot Dog Trail* by Joshua Duder published by Anderson Press, reprinted by permission of Anderson Press Limited.

Contents

How Did You Become a Writer?

Do you enjoy writing stories? Perhaps one day you would like to be a published author? Or perhaps you simply want to know more about your favourite authors? This book reveals their secrets. Through the writers' own words you will discover the sources of their ideas, the places that have inspired them and their writing habits.

Authors are unique individuals and as you read this book you will quickly discover they approach writing in different ways. What works for one writer may not work for another.

Some writers know from an early age that they want to write. Elizabeth Kay was just four years old when she discovered writing and she says, 'I spent my childhood

After I had finished university, I spent an unsuccessful couple of years working in horse racing and riding as an amateur jockey before I went to Paris, where I worked as a bookseller. Eighteen months later, I came back to London to work in publishing and ten years after that in 1983, I became a professional writer.
Terence Blacker

Popular authors like Anthony Horowitz, seen here signing his latest Alex Rider novel, can be the inspiration for some people to write their own stories.

writing about wild horses fighting to the death in the Australian outback, despite never having been there.'

Zoe Marriott also aspired to be a writer from an early age. She explains: 'I've known that I wanted to be a writer since I finished reading my first book, *The Magic Faraway Tree* by Enid Blyton. I think I was about eight, but I've never changed my mind in all the years since then.'

Terence Blacker enjoyed writing as a child but didn't consider writing as a career until later, as he describes in the panel on the left.

You might be wondering what it takes to be a writer. Do you need special gifts? Below is what one author thinks.

Reading a lot is one of the most important things anyone can do if they want to be a writer.

What the Writers Say

'You need a decent vocabulary, but you can get that by reading. You MUST READ A LOT to become a writer, but *anyone* can do that. *You* can do that. The only other skill you need is patience – patience to keep working on your story idea and characters, patience to keep going over what you have already written once, twice, ten times, fifty times, still asking the same old question: could I make this character even more interesting? Could I make this scene more impressive? Have I got the right ending? Have I *really* got the best ending I could possibly have?'
Cliff McNish

Where Do You Like to Write?

Do you prefer writing at your desk, curled up in a comfortable chair, or sprawled across your bedroom floor?

Before you begin writing you need to find a space where you feel comfortable and you can concentrate. Some writers like a quiet space, while others find that outdoors or an internet cafe suits them better.

For Linda Buckley-Archer the important thing is being alone. She says, 'I have two places – my study (door closed) and in bed! I think I need to feel safe and cocooned for the thoughts to start flowing.'

Being surrounded by favourite objects and books can help create the right atmosphere. Tony Bradman explains, 'I have a nice study upstairs in my house – walls lined with books, photos, my electric guitar standing in the corner.' Kaye Umansky likes to create a moody atmosphere with, 'stars in the ceiling and fairy lights and all my favourite things around me.'

I am most happy when I'm writing in my light study in our north-Norfolk barn – a room with two desks, and oak flooring, and brightly-coloured rafters, and long views that I never look up at once I begin to concentrate.
Kevin Crossley-Holland

Jacqueline Wilson likes to write at home surrounded by books.

What the Writers Say

'I prefer to write in my office because there are no distractions. I've got the light exactly the way I like it, the blinds are closed so I can't stare out at the trees and daydream for hours on end'
Michael Carroll

Ann Turnbull also prefers to write with everything she needs close at hand: 'When I'm working on a book I cut out or photocopy pictures for inspiration and stick them up all around.'

Catherine Forde works in a room with a view: 'I have a desk at a draughty window from which I can look out and see birds and buses and traffic.'

For some writers a study at home is not conducive to work. J K Rowling famously wrote *Harry Potter* in an Edinburgh coffee shop and Linda Chapman can understand why. She says, 'I like to write outside of my house because when I am at home I get too distracted by the Internet and e-mail. I often work in a coffee bar.'

Some writers are happy to write wherever they find themselves when the mood takes them, even outside in the sunshine.

Staying at Home

'I have a special room. Just walking into it makes my spirits lift: there are big windows which catch the sun, posters on the walls, and a comfortable sofa in the corner. It's also quite large so I can pace about, which I do a great deal, especially when I'm acting out the main characters.'
Pete Johnson

Out and About

'I like to write in different places, as varied surroundings give me ideas. One of the advantages of being a writer is that you can work anywhere. I love writing when I'm on holiday.'
Georgia Byng

Which Comes First, Plot, Character or Something Else?

All stories have common elements. Characters are the participants in the story. Often they are people, but they can also be animals like Peter Rabbit, or even objects like the robot MALC in Malcolm Rose's Traces series.

Characters make things happen in the story. Heroes and villains are types of characters but often a character will have both good and bad qualities; just like real human beings they can be very complex.

The plot or storyline is the term we use when we describe the events in the story and the order in which they occur.

Big ideas that run through the story are called themes. Common themes include things like friendship, loyalty, loss and courage.

But where do writers start? With plot, character, setting or something else?

For some writers like Nicki Cornwall (right) it is an idea that comes first.

Darren Shan begins with plot: 'The characters always grow out of the storytelling process – I learn about them as I go along.' Caroline Pitcher says, 'Landscape often comes first. A setting may beg to be inhabited.'

I write about questions that trouble me. Why do people fight wars? Why are some people rich and some people poor? But I can't write about a question; I have to write about a person, so I write about a character who has suffered because of things like war or poverty.
Nicki Cornwall

Michael Carroll asked himself lots of questions to write *The New Heroes* series.

The opposite is true for Kaye Umansky who says, 'Characters, always come first. I don't know what the plot will be until my characters are up and running. They decide the direction the story will take.'

Sometimes inspiration comes from everyday objects. Linda Buckley-Archer explains, 'It was a piece of furniture which was the starting point for my next major project.' And for Michaela Morgan language is important: 'Sometimes a word can start things off – or hearing a phrase that would make a good title.'

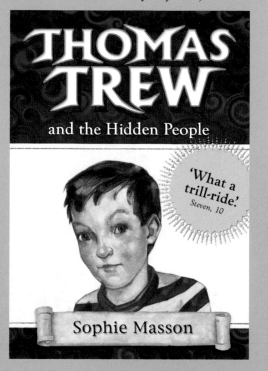

This book all started with a dream that the author Sophie Masson had.

Starting With An Idea

'The idea comes first, and that grows into both the plot and the characters at more or less the same time. To turn that idea into a story, I had to ask myself some "question words". Question words are the writer's best friends. "Why is he the most powerful person in the world? How could that happen? How did he become so powerful? Who is he? Where did he get these powers? Why is there no one more powerful? What happened to him that made him this way?" By asking – and answering! – these questions, I turn the idea into a story, and the characters naturally develop along the way.'
Michael Carroll

What the Writers Say

'Usually I've got a dozen or more ideas for stories floating around in the back of my mind, but none of them have a life until a character decides to live in them.'
Zoe Marriott

Dream On

'It all started with a dream, in which I saw the café in *Thomas Trew and the Hidden People*. There was a long corridor with a door at the end with "Apple Tree" on it. I was attracted by the idea of Thomas the Rhymer, who moved in and out of the faerie world without harm, and who was helped by those inhabiting that world.'
Sophie Masson

Are Your Settings Inspired by Real Places?

Have you ever travelled in your imagination to another time or place while you have been reading a book? If you have, then it is because the author has brought the setting to life and helped you to see it in your mind's eye.

Setting is the term we use to describe the place and the time where a story takes place. For instance, in *Harry Potter*, Hogwarts School is the setting for most of the story. Settings can transport us to other lands, which might be real or imaginary. Helen Dunmore's *Ingo* series is set partially in the real world, Cornwall, but also in an imaginary underwater world, Ingo.

All stories have a setting, but in some stories it has more importance than it has in others. In Frances Hodgson Burnett's *The Secret Garden*, the creaking old house, Misselthwaite Manor, and the overgrown walled garden are as important to the story as the main characters, Mary and Colin. When a setting is really important it may even be used in the title of the story, like *The Secret Garden*. Can you think of any others?

Settings, even imaginary ones, may have been inspired by real places. Kevin Crossley-Holland has written collections of folk tales set in East Anglia and has an affection for the landscape of the region.

The salt marshes, sand dunes, shingle ridges and creeks of north Norfolk: mysterious, sometimes bleak, home to screaming seabirds, always changing, always the same.
Kevin Crossley-Holland

The wild landscapes of Northumbria, like this at Bamburgh Castle, inspired Sarah Matthias to set *The Riddle of the Poisoned Monk* there.

What the Writers Say

'My first published story, *The Frightened Forest*, was inspired by a walk through a disused railway tunnel in total darkness. We had no torches and had to trail a stick along the side of the tunnel to keep to the path. In my story the children trail a rowan branch, and this releases a witch who had been trapped in the rock.'
Ann Turnbull

Beth Webb, author of *Star Dancer*, explains that visiting places helps her to create realistic settings: 'I find visiting a location, makes my writing much more powerful. Sometimes I have changed a whole storyline according to a quirk in the environment – a rock or strange weather...'

And Linda Buckley-Archer, author of *Gideon the Cutpurse*, finds that location research helps her to capture a feeling for history.

Sometimes a memorable trip can trigger an idea for a story. A place that you visit on holiday may well spark your imagination as it did for Sarah Matthias who set her medieval mystery, *The Riddle of the Poisoned Monk*, in North-East England after spending a family holiday in Northumbria. While for Steve Voake it was 'a journey I made across America when I was younger' that provided the setting for his thrilling adventure *The Starlight Conspiracy*.

Linda Buckley-Archer spent a couple of days visiting St Paul's Cathedral and the surrounding area when researching her book *The Tar Man*.

Capture it on Camera

'When researching *The Tygrine Cat*, I visited Camden Lock with my digital camera. It was a bitterly cold winter day but the traders were out in force, standing behind their stalls clutching mugs of warming tea. I captured details: the trader's hands in fingerless gloves as they clutched the chipped mug; the pattern of rugs hanging from hooks; broken paving slabs and tufts of grass that burst between them. Peering through the camera, I saw the urban landscape that would – eventually – become Mati's world.'
Inbali Isserles

Has the News Ever Provided an Idea for a Story?

One of the questions that writers are often asked is, 'Where do you get your ideas?' Ideas for stories are everywhere.

We are surrounded by stories waiting to be captured and written down. Everyday events like the most frightening or the most embarrassing thing that has ever happened to you could be turned into fiction. You might find an idea for a story in a snippet of overheard conversation, an old statue in your town or even a piece of driftwood found on a beach.

Newspapers can be an excellent source for story ideas. You might read an article in a newspaper and wonder, 'Why did that happen? What could happen next?' Asking questions is a good way to get ideas flowing.

Stories about acts of bravery can provide inspiration. Steve Voake was so moved by a report about the Indian Ocean tsunami disaster in 2005 that he wrote a story based on 'some incredibly courageous children who had risked their lives to save others.'

In the News

What questions can you ask about the stories behind these headlines?

- TV Crew find Yeti Footprints
- Rabbit is Mum to Abandoned Kittens
- Humans May Land on Mars by 2031
- Roman Bones Found in Farm Field

(**From CBBC's** *Newsround*, 1st December 2007)

Television news and documentaries can provide ideas for stories.

'*Deep Water* grew out of a news story about a boy whose lies nearly caused his friend's death. I was interested in what made this boy behave in the way he did.'
Ann Turnbull

Pete Johnson also finds newspapers a useful source but says that the best ideas do not always come from the front page: 'I often get inspired by what I see inside the magazines which accompany the weekend newspapers.' An article in one magazine started 'the first whisper of an idea, which eventually became *How to Train Your Parents.*'

Science fiction writer Michael Carroll says, 'I read *New Scientist* magazine quite frequently and I've certainly picked up some ideas from the news pages and articles'.

You could start an ideas file like Sarah Matthias, who says, 'I am always looking for stories and I have a file full of cuttings that I might use in the future.' Cut out and keep interesting photographs as well, as they can give you ideas for creating characters.

Local and regional newspaper headlines are another good source of ideas.

Escape to the Past

'I write to escape into a very different world. I generally prefer books that are very different from the real world around us. I look to history for my inspiration. Not the big famous events, and not kings and queens, but little stories about people who might not have shaped history, but lived through it. They had their personal struggles and triumphs in a different time, but were not so very different to us.'
Marie-Louise Jensen

Homeless

'The idea for my first book, *Vicious Circle*, came from a newspaper article about homeless families in the UK and how social services were sending them to B&Bs in seaside resorts.'
Helena Pielichaty

Is Music Important to Your Writing?

Do you find it easy to write in complete silence or does soothing background music help you concentrate?

At writing workshops, many students taking part choose to wear their personal music systems when they are writing. They explain that music helps them concentrate and get 'in the mood' to write. Is it the same for professional authors?

Some writers prefer to work to music as Zoe Marriott explains: 'I always wear my MP3 player and headphones when I'm trying to write. I find popping the headphones on and flooding my ears with music is a signal to my brain that I'm at work.'

Music can help at different stages in the writing process. When writing *Gideon the Cutpurse*, an adventure partly set in the eighteenth century, Linda Buckley-Archer found that music helped capture the flavour of the period: 'I've written most of *The Gideon Trilogy* to Michael Nyman's music for the film *The Draughtsman's Contract*.'

Although Sarah Matthias doesn't listen to music at the composing stage, she does find it helpful when she is researching. She explains, 'I often put on something Elizabethan if I am researching Elizabethan times, just to get me into the mood.'

However, for some writers music can interfere with the 'tune' of the prose.

> I can never listen to music while I am writing. The rhythms and pitch work against the music of the language I hear in my head. To begin with, this head music may be quite soft, quite hesitant: I listen and try to tune in to the way different people speak, or to the different tones I need to describe something quick or slow, humdrum or wonderful, joyous or sad.
>
> **Kevin Crossley-Holland**

Listening to music helps some writers get into the mood of their fictional world. What about you?

What the Writers Say

'When I'm writing I always have music on. The only time it goes off is when I'm so involved I can't break concentration to put a new CD on. It helps, because it cuts off the real world. It's an atmosphere creator.'
Malcolm Rose

Cut Off

'I almost always listen to music when I'm writing – it helps me block out the rest of the world. I'm currently listening to a lot of Regina Spektor and Belle and Sebastian.'
Sally Nicholls

Rhythm

'Rhythm is very important to my writing and I can't write in one rhythm while listening to another rhythm in music. I also like to hear the voices of my characters when they speak.'
Michaela Morgan

On the Right Track

'I have a couple of soundtracks of favourite songs that I've compiled to help me write a certain kind of scene. One's called 'Fight', another one 'Love'. I also make up a special soundtrack for each individual book, one that I think fits its character. For *The Swan Kingdom* I listened to a lot of folk music. For *Daughter of the Flames* I listened to epic music from films like *Gladiator* and *The Lord of the Rings*. For the book I'm working on now, I'm listening to scary, spooky music from the film *A Series of Unfortunate Events*.'
Zoe Marriott

Michael Nyman, seen here at the piano, is the composer of atmospheric film music, such as *The Draughtsman's Contract*, which inspired Linda Buckley-Archer's writing.

How Do You Approach Planning?

How important is it to plan in detail before you start writing? And what does a story plan look like? Is it helpful to plot 'the beginning, middle and the end'?

There are different types of story planners that you can use when you start writing. You may have been introduced to some of these in your writing lessons at school. Some writers use interactive story planning tools. These help writers to make detailed files about the characters and to think about how the tension builds in different chapters. Writers have different ways of setting about planning. If one way doesn't work for you, experiment with another approach.

Some writers like Tony Bradman (right) make very detailed plans before they begin writing.

Linda Chapman also plans very carefully, writing a detailed breakdown of what will happen in every chapter. But often when she actually starts writing the things that happen change as new ideas come to her.

Linda Buckley-Archer's work as a

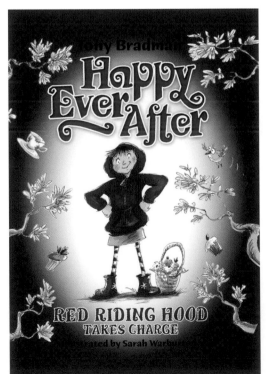

> **66 99**
>
> I'm an obsessive planner. I spend a lot of time developing my stories from the initial idea to a full-scale outline. It's a way of feeling my way into the story and characters and working out how everything connects.
> **Tony Bradman**

Tony Bradman planned this story in detail before writing it.

What the Writers Say

'I daydream, blow bubbles, eat chocolate, go for a few long walks, chat about my ideas with a few friends, visit the place where the action takes place, then sit and write and write and write, letting everything splurge out in no particular order. I call this stage "thunking".'
Beth Webb

Writing down ideas in a notebook as you think about them is useful when planning a story.

scriptwriter has taught her the importance of careful planning. 'To get a good, satisfying structure I need to know the ending so I can build up the tension in stages.'

However, not all writers work with detailed plans. Kaye Umansky says, 'I scribble ideas down on the backs of envelopes, then lose them. I'm not a good planner. I rarely know how the story will end.'

Flexible Planning

'Planning a book is rather like preparing for a long journey. You try and work out as carefully as possible what is going to happen – but you also know that every book, like every journey, has a life of its own. So although I plan out each chapter of a book before I start, I realize this is only a very rough guide.'
Pete Johnson

Different Approaches

'Some things need planning. Some things evolve as I write. Some planning is written. Some is just daydreamed. There are no rules. There is no one best way.'
Michaela Morgan

How Do You Find Characters' Names?

Have you noticed how a character's name often tells you quite a bit about them? You can instantly tell that Cluny the Scourge is a villain.

Most main characters are given names. Sometimes these will be realistic names, like the name of your friend. Other names will be unusual or fanciful. Choosing a name for a character is a serious business, just like naming a baby, and there are a range of things that need to be taken into consideration: the genre, the personality of the character, the historical period.

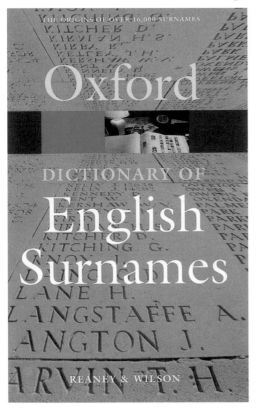

To find unusual names for characters, a dictionary like this can provide inspiration.

A character might be given a name which tells the reader what role they will play in the story, like Tim Lott's Little Fearless. This is typical in traditional stories – Cinderella is the girl who lives among the cinders.

Sometimes a character might be named after a real person. Elizabeth Kay describes how she chose the name Felix for the hero of her *Divide* books: 'This was my father's name, although it was Feliks because he was Polish.'

I came up with the name Dilly the Dinosaur because I wanted a name that was easy to read and worked with the word "dinosaur" so it had to begin with a "d". It meant that Dilly's older sister Dorla could say things like, "Silly Dilly!" as big sisters sometimes do.
Tony Bradman

'I was writing a story that included a boy called Sneezer. Then I decided to go back to the beginning and turn him into a girl: a brave, sturdy, spirited girl with river eyes and a storm of gold curls. Searching for her name, I riffled through the *Oxford Dictionary of Christian Names*, and a pretty, toothy abbreviation of Gertrude caught my eye. Gatty.'
Kevin Crossley-Holland

For some writers like Tony Bradman (left), the sound of a name can be an important consideration.

Dictionaries can help you avoid run of the mill names. Kay Umansky recalls, 'I remember looking up the word "smell" in the thesaurus. I found "pong" and "whiffy". Hence my character, Witch Pongwiffy'.

Kevin Crossley-Holland (above) also found a reference source useful for naming the heroine of *The Seeing Stone*.

Names can have several meanings. Steve Voake explains how he found the right name for a character in *The Dreamwalker's Child*: 'Skipper, the blonde-haired wasp pilot, is the name of a butterfly, also sometimes the name given to the captain of a ship, and it suggests an energetic person, full of life, which summed up her character perfectly.'

If you are really stuck, don't worry – some writers give characters temporary names until they are ready to name them properly, as Sally Nicholls explains: 'Usually when I start writing about a person I assign them a random name, which I change when I get to know them better.'

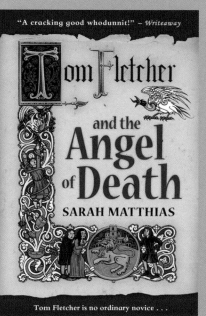

"A cracking good whodunnit!" – *Writeaway*

Tom Fletcher
and the Angel of Death
SARAH MATTHIAS

Tom Fletcher is no ordinary novice . . .

The name of Sarah Matthias's main character was important as it is in the title of her book.

'The main character ... is a thirteenth-century boy so I needed a thirteenth-century name. In those days many people took biblical names and names of saints, so I chose Thomas. I have always liked the name Tom. I think it is a strong, boyish name and my character is a real tearaway – quite a rascal – and so he needed to be Tom and not Thomas. People in medieval times often took surnames from the job that they did, so they would have names like Miller, Butcher, Cooper (barrel maker) etc. A fletcher is an arrow maker. So my hero became Tom Fletcher.'
Sarah Matthias

Do You Prefer Writing in the First or Third Person?

Read the story extracts in the boxes opposite. What difference do you notice about the way these stories are written?

Rescuing Dad is written in the first person, which means it sounds as though Jon (the main character in this story) is telling the story. You will notice that the personal pronoun 'I' is used in first-person stories.

Grk and the Hot Dog Trail is told in the third person. It is as though someone who is not involved in the story is telling it. The personal pronouns used in third-person stories are 'he', 'she' and 'they'.

Why do writers choose to write in the first or third person? Do they have personal preferences? You can experiment with your own writing, changing a third-person story into a first-person story. What do you notice? Which best suits the story?

Pete Johnson thinks that writing in the first person can help capture the right tone in funny stories. 'With comedy, I definitely prefer writing in the first person. Finding the voice of your protagonist is important and when I'm writing humour, it is as if I'm turning into an alternative tone which isn't mine.'

Steve Voake explains his reasons for choosing the third person: 'I like to explore characters and find out what they're up to while my main character is busy doing other things.'

Ann Turnbull recommends trying both to see which works best for the story. Kevin Crossley-Holland agrees. 'The question I ask myself is: what is the right way to tell this story?'

I usually prefer to write in the third person with a single viewpoint. That means you are in one person's mind and see everything through their eyes – so it's like real life. But for some stories first person feels right. I often try out both before deciding.
Ann Turnbull

First or Third Person?

The flight left in an hour. In a few minutes, they would be called to the gate. If he was going to do it, he had to do it now.

Tim stood up. He tugged the lead. Grk struggled to his feet and looked round the departure lounge of JFK International Airport, sniffing the air and wagging his tail.

Tim looked at his mother. 'Mum? I'm going for a pee.'

From *Grk and the Hot Dog Trail* by Joshua Doder

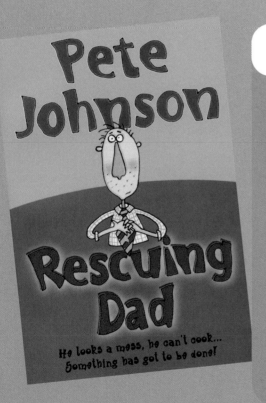

First or Third Person?

It was far worse than I'd expected. I mean, I knew it was going to be bad. But my school report was nothing short of tragic.

I'll spare you the gory details. It'll only upset you. Let me just say that I've never seen so many Ds and Es on one page in my entire life.

Actually, I think I'm pretty intelligent but not when it comes to school subjects. I'm clever in other ways, though. Like I'm very observant. I notice things. I'm sure I'd make an excellent detective or private eye. I started imagining myself solving all these mysteries. I really cheered myself up.

From *Rescuing Dad* by Pete Johnson

Under the Skin

'I have written all but three of my books in the first person. For me, it ensures that I get right under the skin of my central character and see the world as he or she sees it.'
Catherine Forde

Do You Keep a Notebook or Journal?

Having ideas is an important part of writing and making sure you don't forget them before you want to use them is equally essential. To help organize their thoughts many writers keep a notebook or journal.

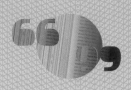

Stationery shops sell a wide range of notebooks, from jotters for taking field notes and research, to decorated hardback journals that some writers like to use when they write a new book. Some writers prefer to keep all of their notes on the computer where they can search and access ideas easily. It's important to find what suits you.

Kevin Crossley-Holland explains that he uses notebooks for keeping 'brief impressions of all sorts. Scraps of overheard conversation. Pressed wildflowers. Lists of things to do.'

For some writers like Georgia Byng it is the process of noting things that helps, rather than having a notebook for reference.

You might prefer to use a computer for your notes like Terence Blacker who says, 'I make notes on a sort of occasional computer diary.' And some writers use whatever is to hand, as Linda Buckley-Archer explains opposite.

Sometimes I'll hear a phrase on a train or in a shop that I like and if I don't get it down right away, I know I'll lose it. Ideas – or glimmers of ideas – can also come to you at unexpected moments; if you don't write them down they might well slip away, just as mysteriously as they appeared.
Pete Johnson

Choose a special notebook for keeping your ideas together.

What the Writers Say

'I keep buying notebooks to write down ideas but in truth I rarely use them. I don't keep a diary. When ideas come or when I hear something interesting, I write it down on whatever is to hand – usually on the back of my cheque books.'
Linda Buckley-Archer

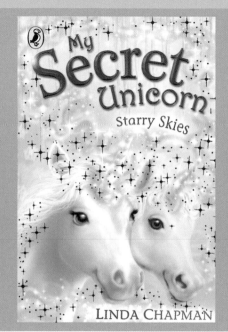

Linda Chapman uses a notebook when writing her many books including those for the *My Secret Unicorn* series.

Playing

'Usually when I am working out an idea for a book I will write things down in a notebook, playing around with ideas before starting to write a proper outline on the computer. I also write down thoughts that come to me, interesting stories, how I feel about things, quotes from books I am reading, notes on films I have seen that have affected me.'
Linda Chapman

A Writer's Notebook

'As soon as I start a new book, I start a new notebook too. I decorate the first page with the working title of the book and the date. Sometimes I'll tape the rough plan I've made of the story to the inside cover. If I make any story shapes, I'll tape those in too. The first few pages are usually filled with ideas for character names, place names, and possibly alternate titles. Then I'll scribble all my ideas and notes in it, make sketches of places or people in the story.'
Zoe Marriott

Noting Down

'I have plot books and they are all very messily organized and difficult to go back to for inspiration as I can't always remember where I wrote things down. But the noting down of ideas and plot flow always helps at the time.'
Georgia Byng

How Do You Deal With Writers' Block?

Have you ever spent ages staring at a blank sheet of paper wondering what to write next?

This is called writers' block and it can be agonizing. Imagine that you have a deadline looming and you can't think what to write next or you haven't decided how your story will end. What do you do?

Do professional writers have the same problem? And how do they get over it?

Linda Buckley-Archer thinks the key is good planning. 'I have a sneaking suspicion that writers' block only happens (to me) if I haven't planned my story properly.'

Reviewing what you have written so far might generate new thoughts, as Catherine Forde suggests: 'I read over what I wrote the previous day and hope a new part of the story grows on the end of the last bit.' Viv Richardson jumps forward to a new part of the story: 'There are always chapters full of action to write. Doing this often helps take the pressure off so I can return to the problem chapter with a clearer mind.'

Georgia Byng finds that thinking things through from her character's point of view really helps. 'I just try to climb into the head of a character and this soon brings all sorts of ideas.'

Sometimes a block is a sign that you need a break. Kaye Umansky works on something else until she's ready to tackle the problem. She says, 'I usually have more than one project on the go. If I get stuck on one, I leave it for a while and hope that when I go back to it, the problem will be sorted.'

Elizabeth Kay offers a different solution: 'A long walk in the countryside works quite well, and so does gardening.'

Blowing bubbles is one of the more unusual approaches to overcoming a writer's block.

One [main reason that I get writers' block] is that I haven't thought the story through properly, so then I have to stop and just think about where it's going.
Tony Bradman

What the Writers Say

'Put what you are writing to one side and start something else. This means you can have several pieces on the go at once – but that's not a problem, is it?'
Tony Bradman

What is It?

'I have a theory about writers' block. It doesn't exist. Usually writers get stuck because they are unclear what story they want to write, or how to develop their characters. In ninety-five per cent of cases, if they can resolve those two questions ... writers' block miraculously disappears.'
Cliff McNish

BETH WEBB

STAR DANCER

HER DESTINY IS WRITTEN IN THE STARS . . .

Beth Webb has a variety of ways to avoid writers' block when she is writing books like this.

Blow Bubbles!

'The best way is to relax and stop worrying. Have some fun. Don't think about your work for a while. Blowing bubbles helps – as does going for a long walk. Daydream, go to the pictures, read a couple of good books, go out with some friends. I firmly believe schools ought to be equipped with pots of bubbles for pupils to blow when they get stuck. It really works, try it!'
Beth Webb

Pen or Computer? (and other interesting questions you may be dying to ask)

When do you prefer to write?

First thing in the morning – usually about six a.m. I sit up in bed and switch on my laptop. I write when I'm only just awake, before the day has crowded into my mind.
Nicki Cornwall

What is the best writing advice you have ever been given?

Dodie Smith, the writer of *101 Dalmatians*, told me that when you've finished writing something, don't re-read it right away. Instead put it away for a while. Then, the next time you look at it, aim to read the story as if you hadn't written it. I've found this to be excellent advice.

Pete Johnson

Dodie Smith (seated) had some good advice for Pete Johnson.

Willy Russell said something really simple which, ever since, has kept me on the straight and narrow: 'character is attitude'.
Linda Buckley-Archer

Jack Henderson of the BBC TV Script Unit told me to look at every single line and say, 'do I really need this?'
Elizabeth Kay

What do you have close to hand when you write?

The only item I need is a good flowy pen (a gel one is nice) and a thick pad of paper.
Michaela Morgan

A bucket-sized mug of strong black tea.
Viv Richardson

A cat. Cats are very polite when you read out bits to them. They are purrfect listeners.
Kaye Umansky

I have a few things on my desk that are silly, small things, but I feel strange if they are not there – a glass dolphin and a glass dragon, a tiny bronze horse, a hagstone I found on a beach and a curled up black cat ornament I bought when I was a student.
Linda Chapman

Do you write in pen or at the computer?

Longhand first and then on to a computer, as I can't read my handwriting.
Caroline Pitcher

Computer first, corrected by hand, than back to the computer for the final touches.
Helena Pielichaty

I usually write in pencil in longhand because I find it more comfortable to sit thinking and writing with a notebook. And I'm a fast typist so it doesn't take long to put it onto the computer.
Ann Turnbull

Kevin Crossley-Holland is the author of *The Seeing Stone* among many books.

Who did you most enjoy reading when you were younger? Do you write the sort of stories you enjoyed reading?

I read very little as a boy. The book I most enjoyed was *Our Island Story* by H E Marshall. I thrilled to her imaginative retellings of scenes from British history. I did prefer myths, legends and folk tales and historical fiction to fantasy and adventure fiction – and yes, those are the sort of stories I write now.
Kevin Crossley-Holland

I loved funny books (the *William* books by Richmal Crompton come to mind) and anything with magic in it. *The Lord of the Rings* was a huge favourite. I tend to write funny fantasy, so the books I read when I was young definitely influenced my style.
Kaye Umansky

I read non-fiction about birds, trees and flowers, such as the *Observer's* books, *Fresh Wood*s etc. I loved the natural world and still do, so I often write about it.
Caroline Pitcher

Do you play any games to help you write?

Often I play a game of Freecell or Spider Solitaire before I begin writing, to help me focus. But I have to watch this; if I'm a bit stuck with what I'm writing, I'll delay starting by playing yet another game…
Nicki Cornwall

Biographies (more secrets!)

TERENCE BLACKER

Author of the *Ms Wiz* series, Terence was born in Hadleigh, Suffolk in 1948. At school Terence enjoyed English but his ambition was to be a champion steeplechase jockey. Before becoming a full-time writer, Terence worked as a scooter messenger, transport manager, bookseller, newspaper vendor, hen keeper, horse-tonic salesman and publisher.

TONY BRADMAN

Tony was born in Balham, London in 1954. He started writing children's books in 1985. Tony is the author of the funny *Happy Ever After* series, and his most famous creation is *Dilly the Dinousaur*. Tony is also an editor and compiler of story collections.

LINDA BUCKLEY-ARCHER

Linda was born in Sussex and has been a scriptwriter and journalist. She is the author of *Gideon the Cutpurse*, a blend of science fiction, history and adventure. She was highly commended for the Branford Boase Award which is given for a first novel.
www.thegideontrilogy.com

GEORGIA BYNG

Georgia is the creator of Molly Moon, the dog who has been hypnotizing readers since 2002. Georgia grew up in Hampshire. After leaving school she studied drama and worked as an actress and children's entertainer before she became a full-time writer.
www.meetmollymoon.com

MICHAEL CARROLL

Author of the superhero series *The New Heroes* was born in Dublin, Ireland in 1966. He has worked as a telegram boy, postman and computer programmer.
www.iol.ie/~carrollm/qp/main.htm

LINDA CHAPMAN

Linda is the author of the very popular *My Secret Unicorn* series. She was born in 1969 in Liverpool and has worked as a theatre stage manager, teacher, researcher, dog trainer, nanny and bookseller. Linda has also written *Bright Lights* and a series written with Steve Cole called *Genie Us*.
www.lindachapman.co.uk

NICKI CORNWELL

Nicki has worked as a social worker, a teacher and a university lecturer. She now divides her time between being an author and a French-language interpreter. She got the idea for *Christophe's Story* after translating for Central African refugees.
www.nickicornwell.com

KEVIN CROSSLEY-HOLLAND

Kevin is the award-winning author of the *Arthur* trilogy. *The Seeing Stone* won the Guardian Children's Book Award and the Tir na n-Og Award. His short story *Storm* was awarded the Carnegie Medal in 1985. Kevin is also well known for his retellings of traditional stories and his poetry.
www.kevincrossley-holland.com

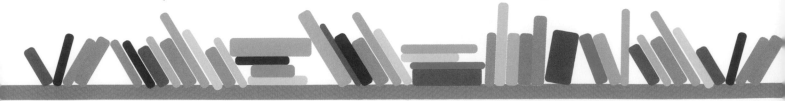

CATHERINE FORDE

Catherine's powerful novel *Tug of War* is set in 2012. Catherine has also written novels for teenagers. She lives in Glasgow.

www.catherineforde.co.uk

INBALI ISERLES

The idea for Inbali Iserles' first novel *The Tygrine Cat* came from an encyclopedia of cat breeds. It alluded to cats in the mythologies of ancient civilizations. Inbali was born in Jerusalem but has lived in England since she was three. She is a lawyer and works in the City of London.

www.inbaliiserles.com

MARIE-LOUISE JENSEN

Marie-Louise was born in Henley-on-Thames in 1964. An avid reader since childhood, she studied German and Scandinavian literature at university and then taught in Germany. *Between Two Seas* is set in nineteenth-century Grimsby and Denmark.

http://home.clara.net/mljensen

PETE JOHNSON

When he was eight Pete Johnson wrote to Dodie Smith because he had loved *101 Dalmatians*. She wrote back and inspired Pete to become a writer. He sent his first story to a publisher when he was 11. It was rejected! Pete worked as a film critic for Radio One and as a drama teacher before becoming a full-time author.

www.petejohnsonauthor.com

ELIZABETH KAY

Elizabeth studied fine art at art school and then taught part-time while her children were growing up. She then studied for an MA in creative writing at Bath University. Elizabeth says that she enjoys travelling to outlandish places and watching wildlife, and she has illustrated natural history books. This interest in wildlife is evident in her *Divide* trilogy.

www.elizabeth-kay.co.uk

ZOË MARRIOTT

Zoe's *The Swan Kingdom* is a retelling of Hans Christian Andersen's *The Wild Swans*. She says, 'The first story that I wrote was about a rabbit and a pig having a party. The second was about a girl who found a pair of magic shoes which made flowers grow wherever she walked.' Zoë lives in a house by the sea with two cats, Hero and Echo, for company.

www.zoemarriott.com

SOPHIE MASSON

Sophie is the author of the Celtic-myth inspired fantasy series *Thomas Trew and the Hidden World*. Sophie was born in Jakarta, Indonesia but brought up in Australia and South-West France. Myth and legend were an important element of Sophie's childhood reading and she later studied Norse, Celtic and Anglo-Saxon, and learnt Irish Gaelic.

thomastrew.blogspot.com

Biographies (even more secrets!)

SARAH MATTHIAS
The author of the historical mysteries *The Riddle of the Poisoned Monk* and *Tom Fletcher and the Angel of Death* enjoyed reading Edith Nesbit, Elizabeth Goudge and Noel Streatfield when she was a child. She cites Charles Dickens as the biggest influence on her own writing. Before becoming a writer, Sarah was a lawyer and university lecturer.

CLIFF MCNISH
Author of *The Doomspell Trilogy* and the atmospheric ghost story *Breathe* was born in Sunderland in 1962. He recalls the joy of discovering C S Lewis's *The Magician's Nephew*, and he knew then that he wanted to be C S Lewis but after finishing his education he worked in computing for 15 years before becoming a writer.
www.cliffmcnish.com

MICHAELA MORGAN
Michaela was born in Manchester but now lives for six months of the year in Brighton and the other six months in the Cote d' Azur, France. Her stories include the *Cool Clive* stories for Oxford Reading Tree.
www.michaelamorgan.com

SALLY NICHOLLS
Sally says that when she was three years old she wanted to be a builder but by the time she was five realized that she would be a poor builder and decided that she would be a writer instead. Sally's first novel, *Ways to Live Forever*, is the story of 11-year-old Sam who loves facts. And because he has leukaemia, he wants to know the facts about dying. It won the Waterstones Prize.
www.waystoliveforever.co.uk

HELENA PIELICHATY
(pronounced PIERRE-LI-HATTY)
Helena is author of the *After School Club* series. Born in Stockholm, Sweden, she moved to England when she was five years old. At school she enjoyed English, history and art and disliked physics and singing. Helena discovered her talent for creative writing when she was an English teacher and she joined a writers' group.
www.helena-pielichaty.com

CAROLINE PITCHER
Caroline is author of *The Shaman Boy* and was born in East Yorkshire. She has worked in a fish factory and art gallery and has been a teacher. Her first book *Diamond* was published in 1987 after winning the Kathleen Fidler Award.
www.carolinepitcher.co.uk

VIV RICHARDSON

Viv had a short story published at the age of ten. *The House of Windjammer* is Viv's first historical adventure novel, but he has also written some brilliant books under the pen name of Ben Bo. Called *Xtreme*, each involves a different extreme sport – surfing, skateboarding and snowboarding.

ANN TURNBULL

Ann became interested in writing children's books when she trained to be a teacher. She decided that she was not suited to teaching and pursued writing instead. Her first book was published in 1974 and since then she has written over 30 books for readers of all ages including picture books and historical fiction.
www.annturnbull.com

DARREN SHAN

Darren Shan is the author of two popular horror series, *The Saga of Darren Shan* and *The Demonata*. The subject of his books belies the fact that he is a very nice person and he refrains from eating children. Darren was born in London in 1972. After studying English and sociology, he worked for a cable television company before becoming a writer. He lives in Ireland.
www.darrenshan.com

KAYE UMANSKY

Kaye was born in Plymouth in 1946. She is best known as the creator of Pongwiffy, 'the witch of dirty habits'. Kaye's mother was a music teacher and music plays a big part in Kaye's life and work. It's influence infuses her writing and, in particular, her dialogue, with a strong rhythm.
www.kayeumansky.com

STEVE VOAKE

Steve grew up in Midsomer Norton in Somerset. His early ambitions were to play football for England and to be a bomb-disposal expert so that he could blow stuff up. Steve's novels *The Dreamwalker's Child* and *The Web of Fire* are set partly in our world and partly in Aurobon where the insects are the size of fighter jets. Steve used to be a primary school headteacher before becoming a full-time writer.
www.stevevoake.co.uk

BETH WEBB

Beth, author of *Star Dancer* and *Fire Dreamer*, was in her teens when she started to seriously think about writing, and had her first article published in a pop magazine when she was fourteen. Beth has been a cleaner, a cook, a portrait artist, a radio broadcaster and a newspaper journalist. She teaches creative writing at Kilve Court in Somerset.
www.bethwebb.co.uk

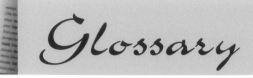

Glossary

character: a participant in a story who makes things happen. Often a human but can also be an animal or even an object, eg a robot.

first person: the person telling a story is a character in it and refers to him or herself as 'I'.

plot: the events in a story and the order in which they happen.

pronoun: a word such as 'I', 'he', or 'that' used instead of a person or thing already mentioned.

rhythm: a regular beat which can be made by the syllables of specially arranged words when spoken.

setting: the time and place in which a story takes place.

story plan: notes and files that a writer makes before writing a story to help them decide how it should work.

theme: a 'big idea' that underlies a story, eg friendship, bullying or courage.

thesaurus: a type of dictionary that provides words of similar meaning to the main words listed.

third person: the person telling the story is not a character in it and refers to all characters as 'he' or 'she'.

writers' block: a state in which a writer is unable to think of what to write.

Index (Entries in bold type refer to a photograph)